Soul Snatch

The Diary... Volume 1

By Ashley Lester

The Creative Rebel LLC

Dedication

This book is dedicated to Brooke Hernandez, Jessica Wade, Renea Boles and Ivory Smith. You four would not let me, NOT complete this project! That kind of motivation is priceless, and I owe this accomplishment almost entirely to you AMAZING friends/soul sistas/cheerleaders! I also want to send an honorable mention to Nafessa Walker. Watching you follow your passion was such an inspiration! It lit a spark to just go for it, against all odds! Thank you for unknowingly planting that seed!

To my brother and fellow author/artist, Marlon Grooms. I used to sneak in your room when you were not home and search for your notebooks so I could read your rap lyrics and poetry. I found it powerful, the way you expressed yourself and inadvertently began to express myself with words to paper also. Kudos to Dianne for giving birth to 2 lyricists! Thank you for unknowingly being my muse at a very young age. Adopting that outlet, helped me in so many ways growing up.

...And in an instant, my life changed

A miracle I call Nasir...

~~~~~~~~~~~~~~~~~~~~~~~~~~~~

Mommy Dearest.

Dear mommy, watching you struggle, watching you fight this

Is a pain I don't know how to bare

And that's unusual for me because I've gained so much strength from losing so many loved ones over the years

I've cried so much; I lost my voice and the ability to produce any tears

But please don't think that I'm not struggling, cause witnessing you fade away is also killing me here

Being helpless leaves me breathless, nothing to do but scream and wreck shit

No matter what I try, I can't seem to crack this matrix

I'm used to feeling powerful now I'm reduced to feeling basic

I keep calling on the ancestors, but I swear I can't hear them say shit

I wish I could reverse it or channel Dr. Sebi on a spaceship

If there were a price, no matter the tag, I swear I would find a way to pay it

Just to see you whole again

If there were a potion, I would find a way to make it

If there were a dragon to defeat, I promise you with bare hands that I would slay that bitch

If we could switch bodies, although I know you would decline... I swear I would make you take it

I try my best to stay strong for you but there are times I just can't fake it

Like right now, I'm letting these words cry for me

Everything you taught me is everything I'm going to be

And I want you to be there so I could see you clap for me

I want you to see what's become of your progeny

Your sacrifice, it made me better

And it doesn't feel fair, but I won't let up; I be damned if you suffered in vain

Nah, I'ma make my momma proud and I'ma do it by living loud

And I put that shit on everything

~~~~~~~~~~~~~~~~~~~~~~~~~~~~

Pandora's Box.

I don't even remember who I was back then…

The days before I sacrificed my soul

The days before I was presented with Pandora's box

The days before I succumbed to being victimized and accepted a life that felt nothing like mine

A choice I would later regret

I wish I had thought about what later entailed

Later, where I have successfully tainted my lineage

Later, when I've accomplished destroying relationships

Later, my body is different

My mind; It's different

It knows lust for things hideous and illicit

Later, I'll have taken 100 steps forward and 200 in the opposite distance

But throughout the regrets of yesteryear

And the later I have yet to meet

Despite all my meaningless apologies and unforgivable acts

I am still unconditionally loved

And I can appreciate blessings at a higher magnitude than most

I am a survivor

A fractured masterpiece… self-taught to master peace

I was broken but I put myself back together like a puzzle, a thousand piece

My torment served as your teacher

Your love and forgiveness became my air.

~~~~~~~~~~~~~~~~~~~~~~~~~~~~~~

The Discovery Stage.

Every so often, a warm light pierce's through and illuminates your cold darkness

Your best days are always accompanied by that light

For there are many days you spend in the shadows, void of jubilee or splendor

Void of that one hurdle you can't seem to jump

The one very thing that sits off in the distance allowing you to see it, hear it and smell it

Tantalizing your senses until you get dizzy and eventually it is out of your range of sight again

The monotony continues...

What you do not realize is, this is all a recycled comfort zone that you trapped yourself into

And the door to this personal hell is unlocked!

But you do not even bother to disturb the door, do you?

Disregarding the fact that escaping will liberate you

You become paralyzed with fear of freeing yourself from obscurity

The conditions are unpleasant, yet you remain a permanent resident of a self-imposed purgatory

Deep down you know your reasoning is impractical

Yet you refuse to consider making moves that are impactful

All because "You Are Too Afraid"

So, you just sit there in silence wishing to be rescued

Knowing full well that no one can find you

And you devalue yourself, despite of the treasure that you are

Never allowing someone to mine you

So, you wait it out and daydream constantly of an erroneous belief

And your hourglass automatically replenishes itself, so there falls no relief

Sulking in your solitude while the whole world is bustling, depriving yourself of an absolute reward...

Darling, there is no future in fearing what your eyes can not see

Step out of that gloom and let down your guard

For the unknown surrounds you anyways...

Disobey the invisible restraints and the false complexities

Realize your vulnerability is not an incapacity

It is only an impairment if you treat it as such

Release your inhibitions and go for what you desire so much

For life is once lived before it disappears in the dust

And it is only worth living if you live it enough

~~~~~~~~~~~~~~~~~~~~~~~~~~~~~

Paint Me.

Paint me a picture.

Take my insides and splatter them all over the canvas

You are so good at turning me inside out

Make me a work of art instead of destroying my rhythm.

My beat, beat-beat, beat

I've been a good girl for you, to you, with you, on you, over you, under you, around you

You have seen my demon; You have slept with her and managed to not be eaten

She never meant to hurt you anyways but still she succeeded and for that I am sorry

I'm as sorry as I've ever been. She's a tricky little bitch but...

Haven't I paid my weight in reparations? Have I not apologized and begged for your forgiveness?

Inside of you also lies an enemy... and here I stand unafraid

When the punishment doesn't fit the crime, the criminal becomes the victim

I've had to turn myself into myself and become someone different

Wear a mask and pretend to hate you when I didn't

Never fully understanding the sentiment that is carved on the flip side of my left breast

Too much power in the message when the recipient refuses to hear what is hard to say

But I've got to say it anyway...

How to explain the unexplainable and define what has no definition

Is more difficult than solving a foreign language algorithm

So, paint me in the reflection of your standard of perfection

Add the good vibes, subtract the flaws, use my tears to mix the watercolors

Use my bone marrow to sketch the fine lines

Use me up until there is nothing left except for everything you want it to be and discard of the rest

Make me the best version of me so you have no reasons or reservations

Paint me pretty, so when I ask the mirror who is the fairest in all the land... I will be looking back at me

I just hope I recognize her

~~~~~~~~~~~~~~~~~~~~~~~~~~~

Prayer does not change things.

Prayer changes YOU and YOU change things.

Take the wheel!

~~~~~~~~~~~~~~~~~~~~~

Holier Than Thou.

I'm a very strong minded individual
So strong
If you don't mind.... I'd like to stay an individual
Intentional about the goals I behold
So please don't take this personal
There's a thin line between being over-bearing and caring
Or satisfying your own personal agenda
I won't participate
And what my mind can't take is your manipulation
Creating fiction from a scripture as if your ill intent is somehow Gods way
Rules of deception outlying and defining
Who has "proper" qualifications to be great
You missed the part that said wait....
ON GOD..... not here to debate
I know who I am and the characteristics HE wants me to have in a mate
Not materialistic... just innate
You lack the mental capacity to unlock understanding of me
Being fully capable of submission
Doesn't mean I surrender my independence
See what you've envisioned was having your own personal Queen Vashti
Hop on one leg bark like a dog with nothing but your crown...likewise AND NOT I
I may not know all the right words to say
When I speak sometimes it doesn't come out the right way
But the same grace that fell upon Moses
Is available FOR ME TOO, so stand
walk upright go forward
His spirit is great within me

So don't limit his expectations of what I can be
I'm curious to know how many souls have become imprisoned
Choosing comfort of what is safe
Seeking him first then he adds to me within reason
This isn't just for me... you like relaxing
It's for all the babies with childlike faith
In a world causing fear of confined space
Don't let them put you in a box
What happens to the purpose God births in them when we cover our eyes to the silent demise of others
Just to save face

- Ivory Smith

~~~~~~~~~~~~~~~~~~~~~

It is the mark of an educated mind to be able to entertain a thought without accepting it.

- Aristotle

~~~~~~~~~~~~~~~~~~~~~~~~~

Destroy and Rebuild.

Patience was your virtue

As you slowly, steadily unraveled the confined

Went to battle, broke down barriers

Fought for what you saw as so divine

Tore through shackles and with bloodied hands you conquered monsters

And other supernatural things that go bump in the night

Fueled by desire, undressed me completely

Exposed the raw. The rare. The flawed. The blight.

Opened doors once unknown... unreachable

Awe crept in.

Branded you as heaven sent

Dwelling in superficial amazement felt amazing

Gliding, skipping. Floating, on pure bliss

Ignoring the warnings, dodging the obvious

Choosing to rest there on that 9th cloud

Caution dismissed.

Gradually the catastrophe blew in hurricane winds

The beginning to an end of an unhealthy tragedy

So very silly of me

Slowly steadily with damaged organs and emotional scars

There is a reconstruction

Rebuilding a wall single handedly

Reattaching the shackles, channeling the demons

Wide eyed, fractured, and bewildered

Dignity, power, and vulnerability are scattered in the ruins

I am beautiful again.

~~~~~~~~~~~~~~~~~~~~~~

Self-Saboteur

The prison we put ourselves in… Only allowing happiness in spurts

A permanent purgatory

Refusing rehabilitation because…

Heaven has no place for the imperfect

Our flaws will not fit, we self-proclaim we "ain't shit"

Instead of accepting that we were born to grow

Constantly running from light…

And the darkness it invites, creates an unescapable hell

The door is wide open

Yet we unequivocally choose to remain jailed

Are we truly un-deserving?

Or are we determined to punish ourselves for coloring outside of the lines

One glance in the mirror and the truth is too hurtful

So, we look past our reflection with disdain and cold rejection

Avoiding eye contact with our own eye

All we are truly avoiding is an option for change

Somehow the truth is unsettling because we find comfort from being in pain

And although the sun shines, we take our rightful place in the rain

Are we truly undeserving?

Or are we self-sabotaging and owning defeat from the mere thought of…

Falling and Failing

O, but what if we fly when we leap?

~~~~~~~~~~~~~~~~~~~~~~~~~~~~~

Genuine relationships are a rarity and life is… well, it's iffy

Do not waste such valuable time on those that are fickle.

Dwell only in beautiful places.

~~~~~~~~~~~~~~~~~~~

Your Inconsistency Introduced Me To Someone Else.

You swear you miss it

But you're so inconsistent.

Why are you so inconsistent, then wonder why I'm different?

Business versus priorities… yea, there's a difference

Home is where the heart is

Can't fake love with an artist

They inhale pain and exhale passion

And wear their bloody, throbbing heart on their sleeve like it's the latest fashion.

Half an effort, leaves me half empty… and my grudge is ever lasting

We could be ever lasting

But you'd rather play guitar with my heart strings

And when my heart screams, you start to twist things

Your immaturity is showing, better lace your boot strings

Because I'm not fragile like a flower, I'm fragile like a bomb

And once you light that match, there is no turning back

the show must go on!

And I will light this bitch up like it's the break of dawn

So, if you can't be consistent

I must remain resilient

Get right or get left.

Pick one and stay committed.

~~~~~~~~~~~~~~~~~~~~~~~~~~~

Maneater.

You read the storylines, heard the rumors

And curiosity killed your cat

Got you hooked on this drug and you kept coming back

Until that sad day when you over-dosed

When my words stopped your heart

When I ripped you to shreds, clawed your organs apart

However, this is what you asked for

You saw the massacre with the chainsaw

You know just what I did last summer. The freak accident with the lawnmower

But still, you took that left on Elm Street… Freddy ran right by you like a track meet

Adrenaline was your Uber

You paid the fare for this affair, now that ain't fair

But your objective was to get here and now you're here

You've arrived!

At your final destination.

One look in my eyes; I ain't even have to say nothing

<u>What a surprise!</u>

You're exactly like the last one

This should be fun

Another redrum....

My thirst for blood is endless

But you've been warned

Persistence has no forgiveness to a Capricorn

Driven by lust yet I robbed you like a thief at night

Cause I'm a rebel now all you're left with is my Poltergeist

And the haunting won't let up, not even in the afterlife

Burdened with trust issues and misuse with every heart you love

Physically with her, but it's me you're always thinking of

The cost of loving a wounded soul is worth your weight in gold

Plus, a tax you can't afford, yet and still it sold

In hindsight, your eagerness was ridiculous

But with a passion so potent and insidious,

No one can blame you for being ludicrous

I clothe my wolf with a sheep, so meticulous

And like Dracula, my glamour is inconspicuous

On the flip side, you were so satisfied

It was a burning desire and you've never been higher

Your fight or flight instinct did not fail

You willingly chose to expire

Your death was so sweet that you'll die again

Cancel the exorcist

So be it; amen

~~~~~~~~~~~~~~~~~~~~~~~~~~~~~

The Epitome.

    Pause.

    Did you feel that?

Did our souls just connect like a magnet?

    Explode... like a silent bomb... totally mind blown

Addicted to the way you move.

  Terrifyingly obsessed with the tender in your kiss
The vibration in your yin causes a frenzy in my yang
  And when that frequency separates, the oxygen dissipates
I'm left gasping for air
  Unimaginable passion radiates from the tip of your aura
Grand, majestic visions of a power source so electric…
  There is a different texture in the air within a 3-mile radius
You and I are a beautiful disaster
  Aphrodite and Hades battle in purgatory
Each defending my vessel and causing palpitations
  Anxiety threatens patience
Don't. Push. Me. Cause. I'm. Close. To. Thee. Edge
  And revelations of magnificence dance in my head
A waterfall holds its breath and awaits to exhale
  An unmoving body of water challenges gravity
The true definition of insanity
  Reliving this moment, expecting a different reaction
A seemingly cruel test by the universal laws of attraction
  I realize your spirit and taste your essence
An undeniable blessing
  Time has been kind, this time
Yet as each grain of sand falls, it feels like homicide
  The love of my life is just barely mine
The volume of this torment is disfiguring my spine
  Be gentle with the execution but please allow a speedy rebirth
Because in another lifetime, I was constructed from the same Earth
  Destined to dwell by your side
We boogied to a tune of temporary satisfaction and misunderstandings for far too long now
  Release the inner matrix so our energies can fully collide
So, we can be fully revived

You see the pain in my eyes…while everyone else sees strength

And I can see you too

~~~~~~~~~~~~~~~~~~~~~~~~

If you force it, it is fake. Let the natural occur.

In ♥ with all things organic

~~~~~~~~~~~~~~~~~~~~~~~~

The most powerful piece in the game of chess is the "Queen"

The only piece that can move all around the board.

Information tells us that over 70% of the civil rights movement and Black Panther party were women.

The interesting thing about religion to me is, how they all eliminate and downgrade the women's role on the planet.

Patriarchal leadership has put the entire planet at risk… in a state of confusion and disarray.

In the animal kingdom, (safari, wilderness or jungle) it is the female that leads, and this is the reason that the animal kingdom is so successful.

Women build nations, men protect and enforce the rules of the nation.

A nation can rise no higher than its women… you uplift the women; You uplift a nation/people.

- Shaun Thomas aka Dope DNA

~~~~~~~~~~~~~~~~~~~~~~~~~~~~~~~~

The Awakening.

Labeled an enemy

Because one look at me, makes you feel weak

It's a common side effect of being in the presence of royalty

Beautiful people, hues of bronze, copper and gold

Like precious metals… Brilliant, Bold.

His-story is ages old

Her backbone doesn't bend or fold

And their offspring will break a mold

They'll be tested, rejected, molested un-protected

Attempted genocide with no justice. No case to be tried

Until we can hear our ancestors' soul cries

And clear instructions to awaken from generations of slumber

Our true marvel hidden

But as the Alpha must start, the Omega must finish

Dismissing false prophets. An end to religion

Uncovering all lies

Drying up tears that fell constant for years

Recycling the bravest energies of lost loves

Summoning all to rise

Conjuring the soldier spirits to again fight the fight

This is the time for rumble or flight

We are just beginning to remember our splendor

And fear can no longer live here

~~~~~~~~~~~~~~~~~~~~~~~~~

Can we just eliminate the word 'minority' from existence? Please!

It is such a degrading and ridiculous term. Words have power and that word is a very in your face play on words. A pseudo intellectual flim-flam!

And if you dare believe that brown people being the 'minority' is even statistically possible, I can sell you a spaceship that can fly to hell.

~~~~~~~~~~~~~~~~~~~~~~~~~~~~~

Brothers and sisters stop referring to yourself as a "minority". Look around… there is nothing minor about you!

- Prince

   (The Artist)

~~~~~~~~~~~~~~~~~~~~~~~~~~~~~

I Wanna Know.

I wanted something tangible.

    Needed something to hold

I craved to know the things

    That no one else knows…

I wanted you raw

Un-covered and up out of your clothes... Free of all enhancements

Away from all your fans and your foes

I wanted to meet your brilliance, and learn all the cheat codes

Put the whole world on sleep mode while I... pick your brain

And beg you to explain

The reasons. The seasons. The how and the why's...

The hell's and the skies

The truth's and the lies. The goodbyes

The visions behind my eyes.

That appear to see things that aren't really there

Should we all be scared?

How does one prepare, when we're all so unaware?

And everyone wants to share... the good news

The news that's not all so new... with numerous deviations

And countless flaws in the foundation

Or have we all been on a mental vacation,

Ever since things went awry in the garden

~~~~~~~~~~~~~~~~~~~~~~

The man who knows something

Knows that he knows nothing at all

- Socrates
- Erykah Badu

~~~~~~~~~~~~~~~~~~~~~~~~~~~~~~~~~~

Through Darkness and Through Life Until Death Do Us Therapy.

Swift thin strokes of blue ink strike the paper

Bleeding out the trapped screams... from scenes that would cripple a weaker being

The melancholy in her stories possess an outlet that feels mandatory

Iron clad guts, still no glory

Plentiful memories that are special, some are gory

some are painful, so they are buried

Some are stunning and breath-taking

Some revealing, some are ugly

Some she'll never tell a soul. Cross her heart and swear to PopPop

Forever mourning Kaiyah, Joyce and Bobby

Bryant, Matthew, Sheed, Shelton, Stafa

Aunt Novella and Maxine

One love to Kairis. Uncle Kelvin

Peace to mama Geraldine

Pour out a little sumthin' for Glen, Jeff, Var and Dominique

The deepest sorrow was the passing of her mother… man that really made her weak

On the outside she is standing, but internally on her knees

In constant prayer, to Jesus Allah Jehovah

For answers, she is incapable to receive

She's merely human yet feels unattached to this world

Her innards are divided into sections, deep and powerful, like the ocean

A stingy lover's slice of heaven

Smooth and rich and decadent

Trying desperately to stay grounded through the super storms

Autumn forever

Craving sunshine with a ravenous hunger

Tugging on her belly from the very core of her spine

Thirst for abundance… and not in small doses

She bravely manages too much to handle

With the strength of a thousand goddesses

To aid in conquering the creatures

That promise to come again

~~~~~~~~~~~~~~~~~~~~~~~~~~~~

While you're imitating Al Capone,

I'll be Nina Simone...

-Lauryn Hill

~~~~~~~~~~~~~~~~~~~~~~~~~~~~~~~

Year 35...

When you walk away

From those toxic ways

And let your soul get snatched

When you set yourself free

No longer a victim of self-doubt

No more long staring matches in the mirror with your worse enemy

When you channel the jesus in yourself

And you take your own damn wheel

Swagger all tall and mighty in your petite frame

Because you can feel it from your head to your your toes...

Queening

Back to loving life

But seeing the world different

For the first time

You can reminisce about some experiences honey!

Not for the faint of heart

Your story is riddled with "Oops!"

And "Un-Uhh, No she didn't's!"

And fairytales with tragic endings

You have slow danced with the evil one of many names

A plethora of Highs in Epic proportions

And lots of low-down dirty lows

Massive amounts of heart breaks

And moments so sweet your tooth aches

So, Imagine the strength of your back!

To withstand and to conquer

You Are A Badass!

Just... look at you!

You're real cute!

But on the inside, you're even more beautiful

Remember to always walk like there is a runway at your feet

And as if you are smuggling jewels at your center

And like you are the strongest entity around

Enjoy the nows

Prepare for the greater, later

Back straight and chest out

Give doubt to doubt

Embrace your fearlessness

As tattooed on your extremity

Remember and never forget

You've totally got this kid

Embody your peace

And be peaceful with other souls that are peaceful

Peace

~~~~~~~~~~~~~~~~~~~~~~~~~~~~

Some Bodies Got to Hear This.

I didn't forgive you until after you died.

Only then did I realize, you were just playing your hand...

from a tricky deck, by a selfish cheating dealer

But first, I experienced disappointment.

The person I once knew and adored from my first 6 years of innocence

Until those drug addicted Vietnam demons came and whisked you away like a bad dream...

You were robbed of your freedom

And we became pen pals then.

But after a while, the frequency of your kites flew less and less

Nevertheless, in the interim I learned you were an artist

And I was so impressed.

And I missed you terribly.

Because I was in love with you still

Soon after, I gave birth to low expectations... at the tender age of 10.

Anger surfaced.

Because why did you do this?

How could you, do this?

I was just a baby.

Forced to live with too many "maybe's"

Forced my hero to be a hero.

Left to nurture, protect, provide and to teach me to be a lady

Fatherless childhood in the 80's was crazy...

Later, I felt regret.

Because you reappeared while I was an adult child.

And although your approach left much to be desired and I basically rejected you. You did try.

I had the opportunity to start the hard conversations, but I was a coward.

The rest of my forever will now be riddled with unanswered questions...

And you won't ever get to hear me say... I Forgive You Daddy.

<center>~~~~~~</center>

Mustafa.

I can't believe I have to write you while you're gone

You'll never hear these words

I'll never get to sing to you this song

And although I know you'll never again be my audience

I've got to heal, I've got to be strong

But I'll miss you

God knows I miss you

From childhood, we've always shared a special bond

From racing down our street, riding bikes and carrying on

Family trips, birthdays, and holidays

To hanging out as grown folk… having sessions

Learned some lessons as adolescence and shared so many blessings

And as we grew up, in some ways we grew apart

But I never replaced your seat

You were the Frick to my Frack

And I, the dope verse over your tight beat

Lord knows I miss you

My heart broke the day he took you

Resist.

Close your eyes.

Relax…

Release what has been troubling you

Give calmness a chance.

Inhale.

Now wait…

Allow your chakras to prove how much of a badass you are

A machine designed to withstand injury and heartache

Hate and submission

Pain and purpose, vassalage and affliction

An intense power… under utilized

Taken for granted

Manipulated into willingly being a brainless soldier

Unaware of your enemies

At war with one another over nothing and everything

Eat the poison. Learn the poison. Be the poison.

There is comfort in ignorance. I get it

But imagine the accommodating honor when you start to respect yourself enough

It's almost embarrassing… the simplicity

All this time you thought 8 hours of sleep were necessary. Another lie.

You've been asleep the entire time

Wake now sleeping beauties

Learn healthy. Be healthy.

Heal thee mind, body and soul.

Be the resistance

~~~~~~~~~~~~~~~~~~~~~~~~~~~~

An Affirmation…

Believe none of what you hear and half of what you see.

Meditate to connect energies with the ancestors for guidance

Fast, detox and eat mostly with your brain

Stretch and exercise regularly

Be kind and question everything

~~~~~~~~~~~~~~~~~~~~~~~~~~~~

The Baptismal.

I find solace in inebriating my senses until I can't tell one from the other

I can't tell if I'm smelling roses, eating them or if I'm being repeatedly pricked by their thorns

When the bottle is empty, I just go empty another

I don't want to feel this emptiness, I need to feel alive

Breathing is shallow, pains are shooting from my shoulder into my lungs

Whatever is inside is lunging, fighting to get out and spilling all over the linens

I pray no one finally comes to rescue this miserable tortured soul of mine

I've already made a deal

Problem is, I don't reap any benefit, so a terrible deal is what it was

But the agony, the faint heartbeat, the blurred scene in my near sided vision is proof that I still exist

Or this could be hell

I guess it makes no difference

I don't remember what I sacrificed... maybe reciprocal love and happiness

Possibly faith in better days...

As I lie still but awake in my bed, only dreams of death and destruction replay in my head

I pray, but I don't know to whom or if anyone even can hear the pathetic

I pray, but I'm not sure of what answers I'm looking for

Or if answers are what I crave at all

I tear at the inside of the wall in search of something more resilient

Seeking elimination because this cannot be life

I'm drowning in tough times and misery and I am the sole one to blame

My own hands deceive me as they force my nose to be submerged in a liquid, could be water,

Probably piss

Vomit in reverse

It's my baptismal

I am reborn

~~~~~~~~~~~~~~~~~~~~~~

Impossible is just a big word thrown around by small men who find it easier to live in the world they've been given than to explore the power they have to change it.

- Muhammad Ali

~~~~~~~~~~~~~~~~~~~~~~~~~~~~~~~

Daydreams And Nightmares.

I met a little girl once
She was running
Running away from trauma broken promises and generational curses
She was chasing after protection hope peace and dreams of self-worth
She was scared
Out of breath... heart pounding jumps out of her chest into mine
I immediately connect as if I had seen her whole life
In that instant.... flash before my eyes
I want to fill all the voids others left as craters of disappointment that she falls into every time......
she comes across one that "seems" genuine
And either knows it's ill intention

Where are your parents
The ones that we learn so early on what it feels like to be loved
Love wrapped in disguise
Living a lie
"She's full of potential" they say
Making less than smart decisions everyday
How can you blame her
Short lived guidance and stability
Draped her in blankets of guilt to cover up their own insecurities
They haven't addressed them
But this little girl forgives them
Childlike faith
Knowing that all danger she was sheltered from was only by God's grace
I asked her where are you going
Who are you running from
She said I don't know you
So this conversation is done
Learned how to be Guarded
They give her candy for her attention
Raise her hopes high for nothing like honorable mention
Cavities are a consistent reminder
Though, so much pain she doesn't wine or cry out
I understand this little girl
Even though she has spoken minimally
It's the simplicity that allows me to see
What she is lacking is also in me
I told her I'll love and protect her
I vowed that nothing will come between us
I'll pour into her all that was neglected
She ran to me
I embraced her
She trusted and could see
Closed my eyes, woke up
Looked in the mirror
That little girl was me.....

-Ivory Smith

~~~~~~~~~~~~~~~~~~~~~~~~~~~~~

How you gonna win when you ain't right within...

- Lauryn Hill

~~~~~~~~~~~~~~~~~~~~~~~~~~~~~~~~

Filthy Secret.

There were times when you embraced the chemistry between us

But you fought it

Wasn't ready for it

Didn't know what to do with it

We've always shared an energy that has pushed and pulled like a tug of war

But then you took your immaturity too far

And almost destroyed us with your filthy secret

It could have been a double homicide you know...

Friend turned foe; Friend no mo'

Be grateful for my sanity

Because a part of me wanted blood to leak

Until I realized you did me a favor

Showed me both hands with the cards up

Dumb luck

Now I know who not to trust

Fuck!

~~~~~~~~~~~~~~~~~~~~~~~~~~~~~

You will never be good enough for a person not meant for you.

Some folks can't recognize your value because

they are selfishly too busy focused on how honored YOU should be to be in their presence.

O look, a narcissist! RUN!

~~~~~~~~~~~~~~~~~~~~~~~~~~~~~

Taboo.

Hard to put in words... and what a shame

Because that is what I do best

Difficult to explain the increased rhythm in my chest

Your presence, your essence

I get high from it.

Our chemistry is our shared blessing. Together we make the 119th element

Where technicalities don't exist... They're irrelevant.

There is no need addressing the third wheel in the room... as big as an elephant

I'm addicted to you and I like to get bent

Let me have another round, it's a celebration love

Life can get you down, but your energy fills me up

On the contrary when it's back to reality…

When we return to a life where you no longer belong to me

And I live with the strife. The very end of empty

Not a wet eye in sight nor an ounce of empathy

Does anyone notice me dying here?

It's cruel how hypercritical people can be

I didn't detect your halo…

The magnetism we possess, is the universe doing a good deed

We breathe life into corny lines like "and then my heart skipped a beat"

We've got the juice that they make movies about.

In fact, we exact the law of attraction

This matter of faction. This, "lights, camera, action"

This passion.

I wonder if we'll ever find out how it was supposed to be… Because, beloved I can't exist like this.

These wounds are killing me softly. I can't resist like this.

The tremors… I can't shake it off me

The things left unsaid, they exhaust me

Can't afford the price of karma it cost me

You Win some, you lose some, but please don't you lose me

I just want to be the cream to your coffee

Your Aphrodite. Your muse.

Your Michelle.

The wish that you made at the well.

The manifestation of the coin that you tossed

The feeling of finally finding what you never really lost

~~~~~~~~~~~~~~~~~~~~~~~~~~~
The Elements.

The rivers pour into the seas, kisses the tips of the ocean and exchanges vows with the gulf
It multiplies itself by one and becomes one
All the while the sun sprinkles its brilliance upon the surface to encourage life. It shimmers like a million perfect stones

The moon creates waves ranging from small to massive and those waves make love to the sand
Gently caresses its skin and leaves its mark of tiny treasures
There is no ending or beginning in sight... It just is
And this is where God lives
In the elements
Water to earth. Earth to water
Giving excellent birth
Providing remarkable affection
Allowing a rise in the senses
Inhale. Listen intently to the melody, Taste nature's salt, Wash your feet like Jesus
Love is in the air
Love is calm and vicious
Perfect storms erupt on the ocean's floor and tsunamis destroy
No warning, No apologies
A lover's wrath
The calm returns and creates once again a soft hypnotic rhythm
A lullaby
Sleep now children
Mother will awake soon and maybe she will be kind or maybe she will rain
Unpredictable, but she remains the most splendid being
I swam in her entirety once. Continents to countryside's
Became a mermaid that befriended a crab and turned little nothings into somethings
I was famous
I was amazed with India's, tantalized by the Caribbean's, bewildered by the Europeans, entertained by the Arctic's
Magic was alive in Africa. Color was sound, and sound was abundant
Energy was transferred down near Indonesia and before I knew it... I sat atop a cloud
And I rode that their cloud from Russia onto Mars
After a brief nap, I awoke with a pride of tigers and hunted white zebra
The ultimate satisfaction
Ripped into flesh, consumed bloodied rawness. Bones breaking under my jaw
I licked my large feline paws clean and flew away an eagle
A thousand journey's later, I returned as a wave crashing into the backs and legs of
Beachgoers in the shallow endings
Playing flip flop with jellyfish
I am everything one at a time and then in reverse
Earth to water. Fire to air. Air to Earth
And then I am technology
A man-made element. Seemingly organic in the 21st century
Knowledge and ignorance at the same damn time
Frightening
Light doesn't mix well with darkness, so it breeds chaos
Hurricanes tore through valleys and neighborhoods
Robbed air from the lungs of the living
Material things immediately lose all value
I pray for a safe return to be one with the wind
The wind that lies atop the water and rides in sync with every ripple
Our humanly love is like the elements
Earth to water. Water to Air. Air to Fire.
Maybe better defined as the fifth element
The beauty of nature
A never-ending story of calm and disarray... Only to return to peace

A sweet sacrifice
Unapologetic, yet magnificent
My rivers pour into your seas, kisses the tips of your ocean and exchanges vows with your gulf

~~~~~~~~~~~~~~~~~~~~~~~~~

Be Yourself, It's Free... and it's not as painful as pretending

Self-Love Note.

I want to hear the stories behind all those scars of yours

Peel back the layers of all the simple ass moves you made in your adolescent behavior

I desire to know what ignites you at night

But I crave to witness your light in the morning

Perfect is boring

So instead of mourning over your skeletons...

Let us embrace the challenges you've faced

And praise how you've learned to implement solutions

I am enamored by the beauty in your evolution

Made in the USA
Columbia, SC
02 July 2023